Date: 5/6/20

J 508.2 SIL
Silverman, Buffy,
On a snow-melting day :
seeking signs of spring /

PALM BEACH COUNTY
LIBRARY SYSTEM
3650 SUMMIT BLVD.
WEST PALM BEACH, FL 33406

On a
SNOW-MELTiNG
Day

To Jeff, who shares the seasons with me

Text copyright © 2020 by Buffy Silverman

All rights reserved. International copyright secured. No part of this book may be reproduced, stored in a retrieval system, or transmitted in any form or by any means—electronic, mechanical, photocopying, recording, or otherwise—without the prior written permission of Lerner Publishing Group, Inc., except for the inclusion of brief quotations in an acknowledged review.

Millbrook Press™
An imprint of Lerner Publishing Group, Inc.
241 First Avenue North
Minneapolis, MN 55401 USA

For reading levels and more information, look up this title at www.lernerbooks.com.

Main body text set in Billy Infant
Typeface provided by SparkyType.

Library of Congress Cataloging-in-Publication Data

Names: Silverman, Buffy, author.
Title: On a snow-melting day : seeking signs of spring / Buffy Silverman.
Description: Minneapolis : Millbrook Press, [2020] | Audience: Age 4–9. | Audience: K to Grade 3. | Includes bibliographical references and index.
Identifiers: LCCN 2019013596 (print) | LCCN 2019017132 (ebook) | ISBN 9781541581180 (eb pdf) | ISBN 9781541578135 (lb : alk. paper)
Subjects: LCSH: Spring—Juvenile literature.
Classification: LCC QB637.5 (ebook) | LCC QB637.5 .S56 2020 (print) | DDC 508.2—dc23

LC record available at https://lccn.loc.gov/2019013596

Manufactured in the United States of America
1-46890-47794-7/11/2019

On a SNOW-MELTiNG Day

Seeking Signs of Spring

Buffy Silverman

M Millbrook Press/Minneapolis

On a **drip-droppy,**

slip-sloppy,

snow-melting day . . .

Squirrels **cuddle.**

Snakes **huddle.**

Clouds **break.**

Salamanders **wake.**

Icicles **drip.**

Chickadees **sip.**

On a **plink-plonking,**

marsh-mucking,

duck-dabbling day . . .

Mist **lifts.**

Ice **drifts.**

Spiders **creep**.

Peepers **peep**.

Lake **thaws.**

Beaver **gnaws.**

On a **hawk-squawking,**

paw-sinking, woods-walking day . . .

Snowmen **droop.**

Cardinals **swoop.**

Rabbits **bounce.**

Foxes **pounce.**

Flowers **warm.**

Insects **swarm.**

On a **puddle-sploshing,**

crocus-poking,

mitten-soaking day . . .

Mud **splatters.**

Chipmunk **chatters.**

Buds **grow.**

Goodbye, **snow.**

Blackbirds **sing**.

Kids **swing.**

Welcome, spring!

What can you see on a snow-melting day?

As the cold, dark days of winter end, life begins to stir. This is especially true in regions with snowy, cold winters. Longer days and warmer temperatures in spring lead to big changes in nature.

SQUIRRELS CUDDLE

Squirrels can give birth in late winter. In early spring, a mother squirrel keeps her babies warm in a leafy nest inside a tree hole.

SNAKES HUDDLE

During winter and early spring, garter snakes stay warm by huddling together in an underground den or cave. Male snakes leave the den first in spring. They huddle near the den entrance, waiting for female snakes to emerge. Then the snakes mate.

CLOUDS BREAK

Clouds form when moisture in the air rises in the sky. As air rises, it gets cooler. Cool air cannot hold as much moisture. Some of the moisture sticks to tiny pieces of dust and turns into water droplets. Clouds form when these water droplets stick together.

SALAMANDERS WAKE

Spotted salamanders hibernate during the winter in underground burrows or tunnels. As the weather warms, they become active. On warm, wet evenings in early spring, they migrate to small ponds where they mate and lay eggs.

ICICLES DRIP

Warm spring sunshine melts snow into water. If the air is cold enough, water refreezes as it drips. A tiny icicle starts with a few frozen droplets. As more water drips down the side of the icicle, it freezes at the bottom, and the icicle grows.

CHICKADEES SIP

Like all living things, chickadees need water to survive. They get some water from their food. They also drink water from melting icicles and snow. As winter changes to spring, it's easier for birds to find water to drink.

MIST LIFTS

Mist is made up of tiny droplets of water in the air. It can form when warm air quickly cools over a colder surface such as an icy lake. As sun heats the air, water droplets change back to invisible gas. Mist disappears.

ICE DRIFTS

Ice forms on the top of a lake when water freezes. That's because ice is less dense than liquid water, which makes it lighter than water. As temperatures rise in spring, ice slowly changes back to a liquid. Smaller and smaller pieces of ice float on a lake.

SPIDERS CREEP

How do spiders survive cold temperatures? Their bodies make a kind of antifreeze! It lowers the temperature at which they freeze. Spiders hide under dead leaves, bark, or snow. When temperatures rise, they become active. Spiders might start to creep across melting snow.

PEEPERS PEEP

As spring begins, spring peepers leave the soft mud or logs where they hibernated. Male peeper frogs gather near small ponds and call loudly. Female frogs listen to the males' songs: *peep, peep, peep!* The females choose a mate and lay their eggs.

LAKE THAWS

Water turns from its solid form of ice to liquid at 32°F (0°C). As the sun shines on ice, it heats the water beneath the ice. The warmer water melts the ice from below. The ice grows thinner and thinner.

BEAVER GNAWS

Beavers spend winter in their lodges. As ice starts to melt in spring, beavers swim to shore to find more food. They cut trees and water plants with their strong teeth. They gnaw soft wood that grows under bark.

SNOWMEN DROOP

You need the right kind of snow to build a strong snowman. The best snow is sticky, wet snow that forms when the temperature is around freezing. When the temperature gets warmer, even the strongest snowman starts to melt.

CARDINALS SWOOP

As winter ends, male cardinals prepare for mating season. They claim territories around bushes and shrubs by singing loudly and chasing away other birds. When spring arrives, they will help their mates build nests in shrubby spots.

RABBITS BOUNCE

Rabbits nibble on twigs, bark, buds, and tender green grass in the spring. As they eat, rabbits are alert to every sound and smell. When they sense danger, they bounce away to escape their many predators.

FOXES POUNCE

A fox depends on its hearing when it hunts for mice and rabbits. It stands motionless while it listens for small animals scampering underground. Then it leaps up high. It lands on top of its prey and pins the creature under its front legs.

FLOWERS WARM

Skunk cabbage flowers are some of the first flowers to poke through snow at the end of winter. The flowers make their own heat that melts snow.

INSECTS SWARM

Beetles, flies, and other insects smell skunk cabbage's strong scent. Flies warm themselves inside the spathe, a hood-shaped structure that grows over skunk cabbage flowers. They carry pollen from one flower to another.

MUD SPLATTERS

In the winter, the ground freezes. When the air warms, the upper layers of soil begin to thaw. Melting snow seeps into unfrozen soil. The frozen ground traps the water. It mixes with soil, making squishy mud!

CHIPMUNK CHATTERS

Chipmunks spend winter in underground burrows. They wake every once in a while and eat stored seeds and nuts. When spring comes, chipmunks leave their burrows to find more food. Their *chip, chip, chips* tell others to stay away.

BUDS GROW

In late summer, trees prepare for the next growing season. They grow new buds containing the beginnings of leaves, shoots, or flowers. When weather warms after the cold winter months, the buds get larger. Soon they will open.

GOODBYE, SNOW

Where does the water from melting snow go? Some of it seeps into tiny spaces in the ground. When soil cannot hold more water, melting snow runs across land. It joins puddles, rivers, lakes, and oceans.

BLACKBIRDS SING

Red-winged blackbirds are one of the first migrating birds to return north when the seasons shift. A male blackbird sings loudly, puffing out his feathers and spreading his tail. His song tells other male blackbirds to fly away.

KIDS SWING

Head outside on a snow-melting day. What fun things do you like to do when spring begins?

Glossary

antifreeze: a substance that lowers the freezing point of water or another liquid

burrow: a hole or tunnel dug by an animal that it uses as a home

dabbling: reaching with the bill to the bottom of shallow water to get food

dense: made of a lot of stuff. A light object is less dense than a heavy object of the same size.

hibernate: to save energy by being inactive for a period. When an animal hibernates, it has a lower body temperature, lower heart rate, and slower breathing.

migrate: to move from one region or habitat to another

mist: a cloud of tiny water drops in the air

pollen: fine, yellow powder made by the male parts of a flower. When pollen combines with an egg, it grows into a seed.

predator: an animal that hunts other animals for food

prey: an animal that is hunted and eaten by another animal

spathe: a leaflike structure that surrounds a flower spike of certain plants

territory: an area where an animal or group of animals lives

Further Reading

Atkins, Marcie Flinchum. *Wait, Rest, Pause: Dormancy in Nature*. Minneapolis: Millbrook Press, 2020.

Barnham, Kay. *A Stroll through the Seasons*. Hauppauge, NY: Barron's, 2018.

Frost, Helen, and Rick Lieder. *Hello, I'm Here!* Somerville, MA: Candlewick, 2019.

Goldstone, Bruce. *Spectacular Spring*. New York: Henry Holt, 2018.

Greig, Louise. *A Walk through the Woods*. New York: Sterling, 2018.

Messner, Kate. *Up in the Garden and Down in the Dirt*. San Francisco: Chronicle, 2015.

Salas, Laura Purdie. *Snowman − Cold = Puddle: Spring Equations*. Watertown, MA: Charlesbridge, 2019.

Sayre, April Pulley. *Bloom Boom!* New York: Beach Lane Books, 2019.

Photo Acknowledgments

Image credits: Ekspansio/Getty Images, pp. 1, 23 (flowers); NAimage/Getty Images, pp. 3, 7; Plus69/Shutterstock.com, p. 4; donikz/Shutterstock.com, p. 5 (grass); Photography by Keith Getter (all rights reserved)/Getty Images, p. 5 (slush); Gay Bumgarner/Alamy Stock Photo, p. 6 (squirrels); Steve Kaufman/Getty Images, p. 6 (snakes); Andrej Kozelj/Shutterstock.com, p. 7 (salamander); Doug Brown/Getty Images, p. 8; All Canada Photos/Alamy Stock Photo, p. 9; Jennifer_Sharp/Getty Images, p. 10; Buffy Silverman, pp. 11, 12 (mist), 17 (forest); Nadezhda Kharitonova/Shutterstock.com, p. 12 (ice); Edoardo Frola/Getty Images, p. 13 (spider); Paul Tessier/Shutterstock.com, p. 13 (frog); Robert McGouey/Wildlife/Alamy Stock Photo, p. 14; Tier Und Naturfotografie J and C Sohns/Getty Images, p. 16 (hawk); David Cardinez/Shutterstock.com, p. 17 (paw print); Jenny Matthews/Alamy Stock Photo, p. 18 (snowman); Bob_Christian/Getty Images, p. 18 (cardinal); Iza Łysoń/Getty Images, p. 19 (fox); Geza Farkas/Shutterstock.com, p. 19 (rabbit); Ed Reschke/Getty Images, p. 20; Danita Delimont/Getty Images, p. 21; emholk/Getty Images, p. 22; Nozdracheva Galina/Shutterstock.com, p. 23 (mittens); GibsonPictures/Getty Images, p. 24 (bike); zhuzhu/Getty Images, p. 24 (chipmunk); ?????? ???????/Getty Images, p. 25 (buds); pixedeli/Getty Images, p. 25 (snow); KenCanning/Getty Images, p. 26; Jim David/Shutterstock.com, p. 27; Oksana_Schmidt/Getty Images, p. 28.

Cover: iStock/Getty Images (front), Animaflora/iStock/Getty Images, (back).